DATE DUE

Demco, Inc. 38-293

D0162692

Nurturing A Teacher Advisory Program

Claire G. Cole

NATIONAL MIDDLE SCHOOL ASSOCIATION

NMSA

Claire Cole, a former middle school counselor, is Editor of *The School Counselor*. She has written and taught extensively on middle level, counseling, and administrative topics. Dr. Cole currently directs the SOVRAC Leadership Academy at Virginia Tech in Blacksburg.

The Publications Committee of NMSA appreciates her willingness to prepare this timely monograph.

CONTENTS

ACKNOWLEDGEMENTS

Two people were especially important in the development of this manuscript. James S. Vaught, Superintendent of Wythe County (VA) Schools, helped me think through the notion of caring in a school and what that means in terms of teacher-student interaction, especially for training of advisors. Jim, a former school counselor and member of the Virginia Department of Education Middle School Advisory Committee, speaks regularly about the importance of everyone's caring for everyone else. He also served as a reader of the first draft of this manuscript.

Dr. David Hutchins, my counselor educator colleague at Virginia Tech and long-time writing partner, and I devised much of the material on active listening skills contained in this monograph. Dave also assisted me in developing many of the advisory activities while I was a middle school counselor.

To both of these fine friends, thanks for the help with this manuscript, but even more, for the many, many years of shared professional endeavors and support.

Claire G. Cole

FOREWORD

The personal-social needs of young adolescents, heightened by a contemporary society that offers many temptations but few anchors, must be addressed by schools. Since the standard academic courses are not likely to deal with these needs, advisory programs have come into prominence as a means of meeting such needs. In fact, a teacher-advisory program is almost universally recommended as an essential component of a true middle school. At the same time, however, it is almost as widely recommended that the implementation of an advisory program should be one of the last steps to take when establishing a middle school.

An advisory program is "different"; it calls for teachers to play an unfamiliar role and one in which they are often uncomfortable; its curriculum is vague; it requires time out of an already crowded schedule; it is an additional responsibility. Irrespective of the validity of an advisory program, such views comprise stumbling blocks to the initiation of advisory programs. Unfortunately, it is true that teachers seldom have had specific pre-service preparation to equip them to be advisors. As a result, many schools that in over-eagerness moved too quickly to establish advisory programs met failure.

Obviously, then, there is a real need for sound guidance and special resources to assist schools in installing and operating these programs. This monograph will go a long way to fill that need. Written by a recognized professional who was a highly successful middle school counselor, this publication provides specific suggestions for both organizing and sustaining an effective advisory program. In addition, sample activities related to the particular topic being treated are scattered throughout. This new NMSA resource will increase significantly the likelihood that middle schools will be successful when they implement a teacher advisory program.

John H. Lounsbury
Editor, NMSA Publications

INTRODUCTION

What they don't understand about birthdays and what they never tell you is that when you're eleven, you're also ten, and nine, and eight, and seven, and six, and five, and four, and three, and two, and one. And when you wake up on your eleventh birthday you expect to feel eleven, but you don't. You open your eyes and everything's just like yesterday, only it's today. And you don't feel eleven at all. You feel like you're still ten. And you are — underneath the year that makes you eleven.

Like some days you might say something stupid, and that's the part of you that's still ten. Or maybe some days you might need to sit on your mama's lap because you're scared, and that's the part of you that's five. And maybe one day when you're all grown up maybe you will need to cry like if you're three, and that's okay....

Because the way you grow old is kind of like an onion or like the rings inside a tree trunk or like my little wooden dolls that fit one inside the other, each year inside the next one. That's how being eleven years old is. You don't feel eleven. Not right away. It takes a few days, weeks even, sometimes even months before you say *Eleven* when they ask you. And you don't feel smart eleven, not until you're almost twelve. That's the way it is.

—Sandra Cisneros,
Woman Hollering Creek and Other Stories.

Who helps the eleven-year-old student feel smart, listens when the three-year-old needs to cry, and reacts with respect to the fourteen-year-old's plans for the future? In many middle schools, the advisor helps, listens, and reacts to a small group of advisees.

Almost all teachers feel genuine concern for the students under their care, but many are uncertain about how to show this warmth to young people. Many middle school teachers feel overwhelmed by the task of translating feeling into action for the large numbers of early adolescents assigned to them. A few teachers do not know how to get along with young adolescents, and more lack the courage or impetus to become friends with their students. Some of us mature teachers were probably taught *NOT* to become friends with students, to stick to the subject matter and leave emotional matters to counselors and family. Teachers often feel uncomfortable when they leave the intellectual safety of their subject matter and delve into the "touchy-feely" morass of early adolescent feelings, hopes, fears, and anxieties.

William Glasser (1986) estimates that the traditional classroom teacher fails to engage more than half the students in most secondary schools and suggests some important ways schools must change to help students fulfill some of their basic needs.

Students have basic needs:

—to belong and love;

—to gain power;

—to be free; and

—to have fun.

Jonathan Kozol (1991) in *Savage Inequalities* describes school systems where large numbers of students seem doomed to fail. Both Kozol and Glasser suggest that teachers who care make a difference in children's learning. Kozol describes the effect of a faculty advisory program in one affluent high school where every student "is assigned a faculty adviser who remains assigned to him or her through graduation. Each of the faculty advisers — they are given a reduced class schedule to allow them time for this — gives counseling to about two dozen children" (p. 66). He notes that this advising is one of the qualities that sets apart more successful, more affluent schools.

Many middle schools use advisory programs to help students satisfy the needs outlined by Glasser. These programs are often called *classroom guidance, homebase,* or *advisor/advisee,* frequently shortened simply to AA or, in the case of the label used here, *teacher advisory,* to TA. The underlying concept is simple enough to understand and accept but one of the most difficult middle school practices to put in place. A TA program is designed to insure that every middle level student is known well by at least one adult in the building. TA programs have as many variations as there are schools using them; there is no one right way to conduct a teacher advisory program. There are, however, some things that can make beginning and sustaining a program much easier, as well as some pitfalls that the wise educator will want to avoid.

This monograph lays out practical guidelines for putting a TA program into your school and maintaining it. The same ideas will work equally well in a junior high school or even a senior high school, where such programs are beginning to exist, although some changes in the content presented would need to be made in high school programs.

1

WHY HAVE A TEACHER ADVISORY PROGRAM?

Teacher advisory programs — TA's — enable students and teachers to get to know each other. Middle level students especially need to belong to a group, one of the basic needs which Glasser (1990) says is met in a "quality school."

> **A TA program could be defined as: an organizational structure in which one small group of students identifies with and belongs to one educator, who nurtures, advocates for, and shepherds through school the individuals in that group.**

A dominant developmental characteristic of the early adolescent is the herd instinct, the desire to be part of a duo, trio, quartet, or entire pod of age-mates. Rarely does one see an early adolescent alone by choice. Some of the saddest early adolescents are those who don't know how to be friends and become part of a group. From an egocentric, self-centered, developmental stage in childhood, the early adolescent moves into *groupness*, a stage that often seems to parents, teachers, and others to be the early adolescent's total focus. As the group goes, so goes the individual, with every group member sporting protective camouflage to become indistinguishable from other members of the group.

Some groups into which middle level students fit occur naturally, such as biological families. Others are institutional, such as Boy and Girl Scouts, 4-H Clubs, and classroom groups. Some groups are highly selective and carry great prestige among young people, such as athletic teams, audition music or forensic groups, and competitive drill teams. Other groups are natural gatherings of young people, neighborhood baseball teams, church youth groups, or religious school classes. Some early adolescent groups are almost entirely voluntary and seemingly random, including groups of friends or street gangs. A few groups have mostly involuntary membership, such as young people in a correctional setting and most classroom groups in schools. Whatever the kind of group, most middle level students are more comfortable when they are with age-mates.

Students in middle level schools do not form their groups exclusive of adults, although they often prefer that the adults with whom they associate not be their parents. We have all seen the strength of relationships, sometimes lifelong, which develop between scoutmasters and scouts, coaches and players, teachers and students. In interviews with aspiring school leaders as part of the National Association of Secondary School Principals' assessment process, frequently these educators note the important positive influence of a school figure, a coach, band director, or teacher, often beginning during early adolescence.

Almost all teachers care about their students, but some do not know how to express that caring to individuals. Sometimes they are not sure that providing love and support for young people is properly their job — perhaps this responsibility belongs to parents or to the school counselor, but not to the classroom teacher. Other teachers genuinely want to express true concern for their students but lack the confidence or words to do so. These teachers are shy or uncertain or uncomfortable with their own feelings, afraid that their actions will be misinterpreted by students or others. Some teachers may fear that they will be viewed as acting inappropriately or even seeming ridiculous to their students. Teachers who do know how to show students they care may feel overwhelmed by the needs of so many students; these teachers may, in frustration, quit reaching out. Who can give true care and concern to one hundred students, or to fifty, or even to thirty? A group of twenty or fewer makes showing more care and concern possible.

Another way of describing a teacher advisory program, then, is: a TA program makes it possible for students to belong, meets their need to affiliate with a group, and makes caring manageable for a teacher, enabling the teacher to express concern in a personally satisfying way to a small number of individuals.

There are times when middle level students need to be in close contact with a teacher for a specific reason. Topics or events sometimes occur which require explanation or exploration in a clear, personal manner — a death in the school, a tragedy within the community, the beginning of a threatening event such as war, an outbreak of shoplifting or violence in the community, a new policy with significant effect on students. If a strong association already exists between students and advisor, the exploration of feelings in areas such as those listed above can be more effective than in a classroom group of some thirty students where the lecture method is the norm. If trust exists between student and advisor, a discussion of shoplifting or drug-taking or AIDS will be much more meaningful than in a classroom where half or more of the students may be tuned out. TA groups with established trust can talk when feelings are high and uncertain, such as at the outbreak of the Persian Gulf War when so many middle level youngsters had mothers, fathers, siblings, teachers, or neighbors suddenly called to active duty.

Thus, a TA group is also a time structure when items of importance, sometimes unexpected, can be discussed thoroughly by small groups with a higher level of trust and concern than is found in the usual classroom.

Discussion in a TA group can also prevent belaboring the same topic or event seven times throughout a school day: a suicide or community tragedy must be handled, but not period after period for an entire school day.

2

WHAT HAPPENS IN A TEACHER ADVISORY PROGRAM?

In an effective TA program positive feelings develop between the advisor and the small group of students in the advisory. The advisor becomes each TA group member's advocate, cheerleader, confidante, and nurturer. Because relationship-building is the goal, a myriad of activities can create the atmosphere in which relationships grow and flourish.

The Teacher Advisory program should be based on the developmental characteristics of middle level students.

In the area of physical development, for example, the TA group might discuss physical changes common to all middle level students, such as awkwardness due to rapid growth and changing body proportions.

Sample Activity

Discuss use of safety equipment for such popular early adolescent activities as skate-boarding and roller-blading. Allow students to present the program and demonstrate safety equipment — unless you are yourself an accomplished 'boarder or 'blader! Include discussion of rules for using this equipment on school grounds.

The moral development stage which gives early adolescents a strong sense of social justice might prompt consideration of cheating or shoplifting.

> **Sample Activity**
>
> Invite a community merchant to talk about the problems posed by shoplifting. Explain to students legal consequences. Explore ways younger students can earn money to buy, not steal, what they want. Discuss how a need to conform may induce some to acquire goods at any cost.

Middle level students' need for autonomy might be accommodated through group suggestions for changes in school rules to foster student responsibility.

> **Sample Activity**
>
> Devise a brainstorming activity where each group of four or five students comes to consensus on three ways to improve the school, with suggestions for how to make the new ideas work. Conclude with a discussion of all the groups' ideas and send them to the principal from your TA group, or invite the principal to the next TA session to react to the ideas.

Social and emotional development may be assisted through community service projects. Peer groups can plan and carry out a project which benefits the elderly or the needy.

> **Sample Activity**
>
> Delegate a few members of the TA group to contact a local nursing home to learn what residents need. Devise a TA group project to meet that need. If possible, arrange visits so that the students could read to the residents, write letters for them, or make decorations for a holiday. Younger people giving of themselves in a service project meets their needs as well as those of the recipients.

Career development may be addressed through a school-wide career guidance program.

Some schools use the TA time slot to accomplish a variety of student-centered programs, intramural activities, community service projects, school-wide silent reading, tutorial assistance, assembly programs, mini-courses, and other such "non-academic" programs. Other schools offer relationship-building activities, such as discussions on topics of concern to middle level students, every day of the week, or once or twice a week. A typical program in a school with TA time every day might look like this:

Monday — relationship-building activity
Tuesday — intramurals
Wednesday — silent reading
Thursday — relationship-building activity
Friday — tutorial or independent study.

The TA group and teacher meet every day in such a schedule, with personal development activities usually scheduled only twice a week.

Another school schedule might call for a five- or ten-minute period every day at the beginning of the school day. On most days it would be used just for administrative purposes such as attendance and lunch count, with the period extended one or two days a week to thirty or forty minutes for a TA program. In other schools, TA groups meet twenty to thirty minutes daily, with a relationship-building or other affective activity every day. However, a daily effort to engage middle level students in significant personal discussion may be too frequent for sustained success.

Whatever the frequency and design of the program, what happens in a TA group should be:

1) Scheduled, so that students and teachers know what to expect and when to expect it. TA should not happen randomly. Left to occur on an unplanned, haphazard basis, sufficient time may never occur to develop relationships.

2) Planned, to reflect developmental needs of middle level students. Just as any other successful school program is based on sound rationale and planning, so is an effective TA program.

3) Appropriate and feasible within the context of the philosophy of the particular middle level school. If, for example, the school is located in a community where most students come from single-parent homes where a working parent is unable to give a lot of attention, more frequent meetings may be appropriate. If, however, the school serves a community where there is strong emphasis on academic achievement and much value placed on time spent on-task in classrooms, daily extended TA time may be less acceptable.

4) Supported by the administration *and* the faculty, so that TA is indeed a team effort among school personnel, not just the pet project of a few.

3

WHO DOES WHAT IN AN ADVISORY PROGRAM?

While a TA program is centered in a particular time slot with assigned students, it should not be segmented and viewed as another curriculum entity. Done well, advisory spills over into all aspects of the school and touches all personnel in some ways. Specific roles for major players in an advisory endeavor include the following:

— **Advisors.** Teachers, counselors, administrators, librarians, and itinerant specialists typically serve as advisors. Some schools include non-professional staff, but such instances are rare and are usually based on the outstanding personal characteristics of an individual, such as a particularly caring school secretary. The advisor is responsible for the young people assigned to that TA group, much as a teacher is responsible for instructing a class.

— **Counselors.** School counselors will receive many referrals from advisors. When a TA program functions optimally, the counseling staff can expect to receive many more referrals than previously, when faculty members were not so attuned to students' needs. While counselors may themselves serve as advisors to their own TA group, they also respond to referrals made by advisors.

— **Administrators.** Many administrative decisions must be made in support of TA groups, just as for other parts of the school's curriculum. Among these are:

- Who serves as an advisor?
- What training do advisors get?
- When and how often do TA groups meet?

- Which students are assigned to which advisors?
- Where will TA groups meet, since there may be more TA groups than there are regular teaching stations in the school?
- What resources, financial and other, are available for the TA program?

While administrators and teachers together need to answer these questions, the principal is the individual ultimately responsible for these decisions.

— Community people. Members of the community — parents, business and industry representatives, mental health workers, and others — are vital parts of successful school programs. Such personnel are invaluable in teaching mini-courses, serving as resource persons on career topics, consulting with advisors and counselors about specific student problems, and providing sites for community service projects.

— Students. Beyond the obvious role as advisees, middle level students can be peer helpers in TA groups, peer tutors, mini-course or TA program presenters, and organizers of assembly or intramural programs.

Sample Activity

Involve all the groups listed above in special enrichment experiences held once or twice a year during TA time. Invite people to teach their particular specialty to interested students, scheduled by interest groups: macrame, bicycle repair, model building, public speaking, photography, creative writing, or many, many other topics.

Often an advisory program is coordinated by a committee composed of representatives from the groups listed above. This committee charts the direction for the TA program, keeping it responsive to student needs and interests while maintaining consistency with school goals for middle level education.

4

WHO IS AN ADVISOR?

Appropriate training for caring teachers is the keystone of a successful TA program. Most teachers readily display their liking and respect for young people. Just as these professionals make the best teachers, so do they become the best advisors. Teachers who do not know how to show students they care, or those who feel overwhelmed by the large numbers of early adolescents assigned to them, often find it easier to form relationships with students in their TA groups than with those in their classes. A well-designed TA program gives teachers the vehicle for getting to know young people through the content of the TA activities. The training provided for advisors shows teachers appropriate ways to demonstrate to young people how important they are.

In some schools, all or almost all professional staff become advisors — teachers, counselors, librarians, itinerant specialists, administrators, dropout intervention coordinators, and other certified personnel assigned to the building. In other schools, only classroom teachers are advisors, and occasionally, only those on interdisciplinary or core teaching teams. The greater the number of advisors, the fewer the number of students in each advisory group. The smaller the group, the better the advisor can get to know each advisee. A group consisting of 12 to 18 students seems to be the goal of most TA programs.

Administrators or site-based management teams should select advisors based on personal characteristics, willingness to be advisors, and availability during the day to serve as advisors on a regular basis. An itinerant teacher, for example, might make a wonderful advisor but might be in the building only part of the day. Such a teacher could be teamed with another to share an advisory group.

The advisor participates on an equal footing with advisees, learning names and finding common interests with students, as they, in turn, learn something about their advisor. If necessary, the teacher corrects inappropriate behavior during the activity and persuades reluctant participants to join in. The advisor becomes the model for playing the game and, more important, for conversing socially to learn about a new acquaintance.

If possible, include special education teachers and other specialists as advisors. Special education teachers often feel removed from the mainstream of the school. Having a TA group consisting of mainly non-special education students accomplishes at least two things:

1. Special education teachers have contact with non-special education students on a regular basis, making them more a part of the life of the school.

2. Students see special education teachers as advisors of whomever happens to be in that group, not simply as teachers of "different" students. The mystery of what happens in the special education room can be dispelled somewhat when non-special education students also go there.

5

How do you prepare to be an advisor?

The best advisors are those who extend themselves to students, not as buddies, but as adults willing to go extra steps, to be available to students when they need an advocate, a friend, a sympathetic listener, an accurate sounding board. Some teachers want to fulfill this role but are not sure just how to do so. Just as training in content and methodology makes a better middle school subject teacher, so does training in listening and responding skills make a better advisor — and improves one's effectiveness in academic classes at the same time.

> **Advisors must know how to listen and respond to students, how to recognize behavior which calls for referral to a helping professional, and how to refer that student to an appropriate helper, usually the school counselor.**

Many teachers know questioning techniques that elicit student responses and lead to open-ended thinking. These kinds of questions also stimulate discussions in TA programs. Some basic techniques useful to advisors include these:

1. Asking open questions rather than closed questions. An open question is one which cannot be answered with a "yes" or "no" or a short answer. Examples of open questions are:

How is your science fair project going?
How could we make this school a better place for kids?
What are the qualities of a good friend?

Statements may also serve in the same way as open questions:

Tell me what you think about the new, longer school day.

Open questions usually keep a conversation going and elicit much more information than do closed questions. A closed question is one which can be answered with a single- or one-word response, such as:

Do you want to try out for the play?
Is this school a good place for you?
Are you in the band?

Note the difference in response the advisor might receive if he asked:

How would you feel about being in the eighth grade play?

instead of:

Do you want to try out for the play?

Likely the richness of response and the amount of both information and feeling revealed would be much greater with the first, open question than with the second question. Closed questions, however, are useful when the advisor wants a specific answer to a specific question:

Did you do all of your homework last night?

This closed question yields the specific information the advisor wants and can then be followed up with an open question to gain yet more information:

How did you go about arranging your time last night to get everything done, since you had been having trouble completing everything before? We want to repeat this success!

2. Reflecting student's thoughts. Another useful technique is that of reflection, restating the content so that the student continues to give more information or feelings on the same topic. The student might say,

I felt rotten when I found out my dad wouldn't let me go on the trip with the other kids.

The advisor might respond with,

You felt awful?
or
Your dad wouldn't let you go?

Chances are a student making such a statement wants to continue talking about the topic and this type of response invites further comments. Often a middle schooler wants to tell a sympathetic listener whatever is uppermost in his/her mind. The advisor can shape the conversation by which part of the sentence he reflects: the feeling (*rotten*); the event (*trip*); the people involved (*Dad, other kids*); or any other part of the student's statement.

The skilled advisor knows that moralizing or *platitudinizing* kills a conversation quickly: "You know your dad knows best" will not build much of a relationship between advisor and advisee, even if the advisor does know that the father is right in this case. The advisor does not need to take sides or moralize to keep the conversation going and find out how the student feels about the situation. If the student asks directly, of course, honesty impels the advisor either to give an opinion or tell the student that he has no opinion or will not give one in this particular situation. Generally, however, the student is much more interested in giving views than in hearing the advisor's perspective on a given topic. Simply listening attentively and non-judgmentally to young people is a great beginning to building trust.

3. Using silence. Teachers familiar with questioning techniques know the value of "wait time" and the difficulty in letting silence hang while a student frames (or avoids!) an answer. Particularly in conversation related to feelings and thoughts, advisors must give sufficient "wait time" for their advisees to respond. Silence is a great probe: most of us feel compelled to make silence go away, so we begin talking. Usually a teacher fills the silence first; the effective advisor will learn to be comfortable enough with silence so a student can fill the conversational lull, rather than the advisor. Practice in letting silence stretch for five, ten, or even twenty seconds will allow the advisor to feel more comfortable with quiet during a conversation.

These three basic, easy-to-acquire techniques of asking open questions, reflecting thoughts and feelings, and using silence will make advisors much more effective listeners. Teachers can practice these listening skills in workshops as they prepare to become advisors. In *Helping Relationships and Strategies,* Hutchins and Cole (1991) discuss these and other useful techniques further and give many suggestions for practice.

Advisors also need to learn to recognize aberrant behavior in young people. School counselors, while well-trained in this area, do not see youngsters on the same day-to-day basis that advisors do and depend on advisors to pick up patterns of behavior. For example, an advisor may be the first person to notice anti-social or fearful behavior that may indicate sexual abuse of a pubescent girl with a new stepfather. Or the advisor may note a pattern of lateness to school, fogginess of response, failing grades, and association with new friends that may suggest substance abuse. The advisor, just as every other professional, will be careful not to leap to conclusions based on frail evidence. However, the advisor should be the person in the school who knows her advisees better than anyone else and detects changes in behavior which signal difficulty.

Advisors do not need to know how to solve all their advisees' problems, but they must know how to refer them to others who can help. The need for confidentiality must be respected. The referral routes and resources vary from school to school. Some schools will have a resident school nurse, while others may not even have ready access to a health professional. Middle level counselors and administrators are always a prime referral resource for advisors, as are colleagues on a teaching team willing to talk over an advisee's behavior. Some systems have substance abuse counselors or dropout prevention specialists; most have learning specialists — special education or gifted resource teachers — who will discuss early adolescents' learning problems.

Advisors do not function alone in a middle school, any more than do other teachers. Other staff members are available to help advisors consider special needs of their advisees and to marshall resources. The advisor must not consciously overlook student needs on the theory that it's someone else's responsibility. Knowing the advisee better than anyone else in the school and doing whatever is necessary for that individual to function optimally in the school *is* the advisor's responsibility.

Some teachers simply are not willing or able to enter into the kind of a relationship with students that is needed for an effective TA program. In such rare instances, the school administrator may arrange an alternate assignment.

6

WHAT KINDS OF ACTIVITIES WORK BEST?

A teacher advisory program is both a concept of relationship-building and a time structure within a school day. How the school views these two aspects of the TA program will determine what happens during TA time.

Some schools use the TA time to conduct a variety of activities: sustained silent reading, intramural events, community service projects, current events discussion, special interest mini-courses, relationship-building programs, assemblies, administrative details, and a host of other things. The philosophy of the school and the TA program determines the activities and the frequency of meetings. *Treasure Chest* (Hoversten, Doda, and Lounsbury, 1991), a previously cited source book for TA activities, contains 120 examples of many types of activities.

In many schools, TA happens several times a week, sometimes for varying lengths of time. In some schools, for example, students meet with their advisor daily for a few minutes of typical homeroom details (attendance, lunch count, daily announcements), with an extended time for some kind of TA activity one or two days a week. While the briefer time is not long enough for any kind of meaningful relationship-building, the student touches base with the advisor daily and every student has a homebase.

Virtually every successful program includes group activities for students and teachers to get to know one another and to discuss ideas of importance to them. Some schools use a particular program such as "Quest" developed by the Lions Club. Others devise their own TA program, usually borrowing heavily from other successful programs which have shared materials.

ACTIVITIES TO BUILD RELATIONSHIPS

Typical kinds of activities which encourage relationship-building in a TA program include personal concerns of students, instructional concerns, school concerns, and career education.

1. Personal concerns of students. Middle level young people like to know something about the group they are with and the teacher before them. Because being a part of the peer group is so important, they need to know who else is in the group. Few things are as scary in life as entering a new school, even with a group the student has known since kindergarten days. Consider entering a school in a new community or in the middle of the year, when being new assumes gargantuan proportions for some students. Scheduling a number of get-acquainted activities is always a good idea. The sooner the advisor gets to know names and something about each student, the better. As new students enter the group and as students "discover" each other during the school year, the group can use variations of this type of activity.

Students like to know what is happening to them and how to handle new thoughts and feelings. While the typical TA group is not where the teacher wants to get into a technical discussion of sexual maturation, feelings associated with becoming adolescent are surely appropriate topics for discussions with TA groups after some trust has built between advisor and students. Most pre- and early adolescents are experiencing some degree of conflict in home and peer relationships and are eager to talk about how to get along better with most everyone in the world.

Other topics of interest to students fall under the general heading of societal concerns as they personally relate to students: divorce, substance abuse, peer influence, shoplifting, individual differences, handicapping conditions, cultural diversity, and other such areas. In most communities, divorce, remarriage, blended families, and various family configurations pose concerns for early adolescents. Some opportunity to talk about what it's like to be in a family different from the "traditional" one — which may well not be the dominant pattern in the community — will interest students. Likewise, how does a family change when a grandparent or other elderly person comes in to live, or when an older sibling returns home? A TA program on handicapping conditions — Just what is a learning disability? How is life different in a wheelchair or a neck brace? — can sensitize an early adolescent to personal differences in people.

Sample Activity

Ask students to consider questions such as:

How would your life be different if you were
- shorter/taller?
- older/younger?
- a different gender?
- a different culture or ethnic group?
- unable to walk/talk/hear/see/speak English?

Conduct a discussion on valuing differences in people, building on strengths, and accepting what is unchangeable in life, such as genetic short stature.

The personal concerns of students is a broad category that will vary by school, grade, geographic region, ethnic group, and community situation. The area of activity, however, holds great appeal for students in middle level TA programs.

2. Instructional concerns. Instruction is the *raison d'etre* of the middle school, and TA programs have a definite role to play in the instructional process. Many areas relating to instruction can be handled between advisor and student, including discussion of grades, course selection, study skills, availability of tutorial help, preparation for standardized testing, and other such topics.

In a middle school, sometimes no one adult considers a student's entire report card until the counselor or principal has a chance to look at each student's grades — which can be a considerable time after marks are recorded. The advisor can quickly scan the report cards of all persons in the advisory and have a short conference with every advisee within a short time soon after report cards have been issued. Thus, every student almost immediately can have individual feedback to receive praise for good grades and help in planning how to improve poor ones.

Most middle level schools offer some electives to students. While counselors usually meet with students and their parents to help with these choices, the advisor, who knows the student best, also has a role.

High school counselors can meet with eighth grade students in their TA groups to talk about requirements and course options available in the high school. Typically, students need to hear this information more than once. The advisor who has also listened to the high school counselor can help to clarify many remaining questions. The advisor may not want to lead a student to decide which mathematics class to take, but can raise appropriate questions and explain a credit or Carnegie unit. The advisor who knows the student's abilities, interests, aspirations, and achievement through an extended relationship in the TA group is in an excellent position to advise on course selection and implications for future career and educational decisions.

Many students in middle schools need help in developing good study skills. Some TA programs routinely include this topic for their students; other schools include such instruction within core curriculum classes. Advisors can also help students get the tutorial assistance they need from other teachers, peer tutors, or parent/community volunteers.

Sample Activity

Devise a form for each advisee to chart study time and conditions over a period of several days (where, what distractions such as radio, TV, guests, what resources were available such as computer or encyclopedia). Review the chart with each individual to decide what might be the optimum study conditions for that person. The advisor might also learn that an advisee who lives in a crowded apartment and has child-care responsibility for younger siblings needs study time and space within the school day, rather than at home.

Standardized testing is a fact of life in most schools, with both student and school success judged heavily by student performance on a variety of tests. TA activities can help prepare students for such tests by discussing the importance of testing, providing test-taking strategies, and holding discussions with a small group of students to build more positive attitudes toward testing. Students can complete interest inventories in TA groups and receive interpretations from their advisor or from the counselor coming into the small TA group to discuss scores with students.

Sample Activity

Bring several old neckties to school — the more garish and outmoded, the better. Ask five or six volunteers to stand before the group and tie the ties, giving no instruction on what the tied necktie should look like. When all are tied, ask the group to vote on which is best. Then discuss what standard was used in deciding what constitutes the best tie: is there a generally recognized tie-tying standard? Talk about creativity and previous experience with neckties. Relate this concrete example to how norms are developed for standardized tests, and how judgments are made about students' achievements using normed tests.

---

3. School concerns. For all students, there are school-related concerns that students want to discuss or teachers and administrators want them to discuss. Among these are school rules and regulations, orientation information such as who to see for what, attendance procedures, personnel in the school, registration for the next year, and other such topics.

Almost every middle school has a student handbook which contains rules, procedures, and discipline policies. TA is the ideal place to discuss those regulations because the advisor can be sure everyone in the small group understands behavior expectations and consequences for infringement. It is a good idea to hold these discussions more than once during the year, especially if it becomes apparent that particular behaviors need more attention. If fighting becomes widespread in the school, TA groups can discuss ways to settle conflicts other than by hitting. Also, advisors can thoroughly explain policies such as attendance and tardy regulations. Students must understand how the school operates and what procedures are in place. TA is a good time to discuss how to check out of school for a dental appointment; who the sixth grade counselor is and how to get an appointment; where the library, gym, cafeteria, and school store are located; how student council operates; who can play intramurals; and other such school procedures students need to understand.

Sample Activity

Devise a quiz on pertinent information about the school — people, procedures, places, and other such information. Divide the TA group into teams and give the questions in spelling bee fashion, with the entire team, not an individual, supplying the answer. Discuss with students any information which seems unclear or unfamiliar to them.

Some students need special help from the school. The advisor may learn that Sara doesn't take band because her family can't afford to rent an instrument, but she'd really like to learn to play trombone. Issues of free lunch, clothing, and perhaps even shelter and safety may come first to the attention of the advisor, who learns that a sleepy student has spent the last several nights in a car because the family has nowhere else to live. Because advisors know their advisees better than anyone else in the building, the advisors often become the first line of referral. The advisor does not become responsible for clothing a child — although this often happens — but rather for referring the child to a helping person, usually the school counselor, who knows how to arrange for this assistance.

Sometimes a school problem will emerge which advisors can most efficiently deal with. Suppose, for example, tardiness to class is rampant, defying efforts to clear the halls into classrooms in the appointed class changing time. As adults we often assume that students know how to get around the building efficiently; in reality, they often go to their lockers much more frequently than necessary and do not always know the best route between two parts of the building. Administrators and counselors are well aware of parent complaints that their children never have time to go to the bathroom between classes for fear of tardiness.

Sample Activity

Make a map of the school, or of the portion of the school traveled by a particular TA group. Ask each student to plot a route around the school, noting locker stops, perhaps library visit time, and bathroom stops. Discuss with each student when he needs to visit his locker — before lunch to pick up his lunch, or can he carry that to his third hour class, eliminating that stop? When does the saxophone player go to the band room to pick up her instrument to take home to practice?

While the exercise may help only a few, considering passage through the building in a TA activity puts a more positive note on solving a problem than simply thinking up new punishments to serve as deterrents.

4. Career education. Middle level students are at an ideal time developmentally for career education. They want things and begin to understand the need to earn, as parents preach about money and its use. They begin to have sustained career interests and can understand that, if they are good in mathematics, some career areas such as engineering or bookkeeping may be more appealing to them.

TA is a good place to include career exploration activities. Using speakers, videotapes, and print materials an entire group might decide to explore a career area, such as careers in the entertainment industry. Or each group in a grade might invite a career speaker and the students regroup to rooms to hear the speaker of most interest to them. All students in a grade might take a career interest inventory through the group, with interpretation by the advisor or the counselor. TA might become the vehicle for a career fair, using TA groups as the place to conduct the interest survey and giving explanations to students about procedures.

Sample Activity

Ask TA group members to survey five adults each to find out why they work and how they got into the job they currently have. Discuss the answers, exploring how some people plan and prepare for jobs and others just wander into them without prior planning. Emphasize the value of planning and acquiring an education for optimum career development.

---

5. Other areas. As many other kinds of activities fit into a TA program as there are special needs and special interests of schools. From naming TA's to designing school T-shirts to community or school service projects to mandated AIDS education, the topics and ways of delivering the topics are limited only by time and advisor imagination.

Occasionally changes in a school mean explaining something to all students quickly and well. At such times a TA program becomes invaluable. If a class of trainable mentally retarded children became a part of the school, for example, a TA program to explain how the children are handicapped, how the main student body can help the new students, and other such information can decrease the discomfort students at this particular developmental stage of their lives feel upon seeing peers who are decidedly different from themselves. One school suddenly faced with helping two children experiencing daily epileptic seizures quickly developed a TA program to deliver epilepsy awareness to all students and teachers in the building. The TA groups provided a ready access to all in a very short time span.

When a crisis hits a school, such as the death of a student or faculty member or other community tragedy, the TA group may become literally a lifesaver as all students have an immediate way of talking about the incident in a place where they already belong, with an adult whom they trust. In such a situation as the death of a student or faculty member, students need to express their feelings and plan a memorial. When an advisor and a group of students have established trust and discussed feelings and thoughts in the past, such a discussion is much easier than in a large group where teacher-directed activity has been the norm.

When the Gulf War broke out in 1990, schools with functional TA programs doubtless had a better way of helping students understand what was happening than those without, as early adolescents experienced parents, siblings, and teachers leaving with reserve units. Additionally, talking about something in TA groups can relieve the need to do so period after period after period all day long. Everyone knows the topic has been pursued by all students already, and regular instruction can go on throughout the rest of the day, providing familiar structure at a crisis time when students most need normalcy. Consider the following situation.

Sample Activity

Because a storm heavily damaged a nearby middle level building, a large group of students will be attending your school temporarily, This will cause very crowded conditions. Traditional rivalry exists between the two student bodies. TA groups become the ideal vehicle to inform students quickly about what is to happen and how their lives will change temporarily. Each TA group can discuss ways to ease the crowding and welcome the visiting students. Students should explore how they might feel if the situation were reversed.

The faculty and administration have an excellent vehicle for addressing any problem or concern that might arise during the year when the school has already established TA groups. Surprisingly serious and productive discussions of school problems can and do occur in these intimate, small groups — and real solutions emerge.

7

WHAT ARE SOURCES FOR ADVISORY ACTIVITIES?

TA activities and topics must be based on developmental needs of students. The goals of the TA program should determine the activities. What do you want the TA program to accomplish: relationship-building only? a specific set of content objectives? a variety of things such as intramurals, tutorial, silent reading? Your decisions about the goals of the program will define both the topics to be covered and the activities which address those topics. Methods of delivery include the same attention to group work, physical movement, cognitive level, and teacher preparation as any other middle school lesson.

Some schools purchase a commercially prepared set of lessons to comprise the teacher advisory curriculum. While such programs can be valuable resources, they do not address the specific concerns of an individual school or a particular group of students. Also, the professional staff loses the valuable team-building experiences which occur as a faculty determines what will happen during TA time. Too often, commercial programs rely heavily on paper-and-pencil activities, and the best TA programs shy away from these on a regular basis. Most schools devise their own activities, borrowing heavily from other schools' successful programs and purchased materials. This way topics and activities can be tailored to that specific school and its objectives.

In most middle level schools, one person, often a counselor, coordinates the TA program and prepares optional activities to be used in TA groups. Teachers rarely feel they have time to devise TA activities, and teacher acceptance of TA is far greater if there is not extra lesson preparation. A teacher or other staff member can assume this responsibility, but it should be recognized that it will take significant time. Advisors are generally much more enthusiastic about TA if they receive whatever they need to conduct a particular activity instead of having to prepare the materials themselves: enough copies of student worksheets, materials for a community service project, sports equipment for intramurals, videotape for a career education presentation, or whatever material is required for a particular TA activity. As programs mature and teachers become more comfortable in the role of advisor, there is less need to depend on pre-planned activities.

In many schools, a committee of staff members interested in TA programs provides ongoing direction and monitoring of the program. The committee may, for example, set topics for a month, with suggestions for activities. The theme for September might logically be "getting acquainted," using activities such as paired introductions, a Bingo-type game of meeting new people, a mnemonic game to learn names, a self-collage made of magazine pictures or photos brought from home, or any of a host of other activities, limited only by the teacher's imagination. The theme for October might be educational excellence, with emphasis on study skills, review of the first marking period's report card, test-taking skills, information on how to access tutorial assistance, and other related topics.

Sample Activity

Ask students to introduce themselves using their first names and an adjective beginning with the same sound to describe themselves, such as "Powerful Paul" or "Jivey Jonica." Each student says her own name and then repeats the names of everyone who has gone before her. The advisor may need to supply adjectives — positive, of course — for some of the participants.

A TA activity can be developed using popular music. A good stimulus for an activity is a selection from contemporary music, such as Randy Travis' "Heroes and Friends." An advisor can lead a discussion on the qualities of friendship, adolescent heroes and how they are created, or any of a number of areas suggested by this piece of music. Students relate to contemporary music easily, but advisors must be sure that they and the students understand lyrics in the same manner — some lyrics have specialized meanings for young people which adults may not understand.

Other sources for TA activities include television programs, especially those about young people, which can be used as videos; movies about early adolescent concerns, readily available through your local video store (screen them carefully yourself first!); local news events; and national events such as Earth Day or Black History Month. *Treasure Chest: A Teacher Advisory Source Book* (Hoversten, Doda, and Lounsbury, 1991, p. 11) lists twenty-one books suitable for reading aloud with a TA group with discussion following.

TA programs should not rely on paper and pencil activities. Certainly advisors can learn something about their advisees from what the students write, but relationships are not built primarily through the written word. Activities should be designed for maximum interaction between advisor and advisees, preferably in an informal atmosphere where free exchange of thoughts and ideas can occur. As one teacher has said, "Take the PP out of AA" — use something other than paper and pencil activities most of the time.

Some schools have set up TA programs which are primarily "rap sessions." While such a program can be successful with older adolescents in a high school, early adolescents generally need a more structured program than a free-flowing, name-your-own topic session every day. There is surely a time and a place for an unplanned topic which arises from the moment, but usually TA sessions should be planned with the same care and attention as any other class offering.

8

WHAT ARE ADMINISTRATIVE CONSIDER-ATIONS IN ESTABLISHING A PROGRAM?

When beginning an advisory program many matters will call for decisions by the principal, often working with the committee who plans the program. Among these are: How will students be assigned to advisors? Who will serve as teacher advisors? Where will TA groups meet? When and how often will TA groups be scheduled? What budget will be required for TA activities? How will the program be presented to the school publics—parents, school board, entering students, feeder, and receiving schools?

1. How will students be assigned to advisors? Different methods can be used for assigning students to advisors. Some schools group students across grades, so that in a 6-8 school, one-third of a group (the eighth graders) leave each year and one-third come in new (the sixth graders). Advantages of this method are that students stay with the same advisor for three years, and sixth graders receive some "protection," as well as advice, from the seventh and eighth graders. However, students must be regrouped from time-to-time in such an arrangement. For example, eighth graders need orientation to the high school and sixth graders must learn about the middle school. In other schools, students stay with the same advisor for three years; advisor and students advance together and remain together. In both of these assignment methods, an advisor and advisees remain together for the duration of the students' middle grade years.

Students are sometimes assigned by alphabet, or at random by the computer. In a few schools, students select their advisors after the first year, listing multiple choices so that the staff can place everyone with one of his/her choices. Some schools intentionally distribute students with leadership talent and those with behavior problems throughout the groups and fill everyone else in around them. Some schools use a "draft system" with teachers selecting those students with whom they think they can work the best. Whatever method is used, administrators should give serious consideration to having students remain with the same advisor as many years as possible in the middle school.

2. Who will serve as teacher advisors? Most TA programs try to involve as many professional staff as possible as advisors to reduce the number of students assigned to each group. Between twelve and twenty students seem to be a generally accepted number for a good-sized TA group. The more staff involved, the fewer the students in each group. The administrator must consider who will be a good advisor when making those assignments.

In some schools, *all* staff have a TA group — administrators, librarians, counselors, teachers, and any other professional staff in the building. In other schools, at least one person, usually an administrator, is not assigned a group in order to run the school during TA time. Sometimes an additional staff member, often a counselor, is assigned the responsibility for running the TA program, and therefore is not assigned a group. The program coordinator can then step in to take a group in an emergency situation, such as a somewhat sensitive discussion when a substitute is in the room; to model how a TA group can function effectively for a advisor having trouble with a group; or to handle details of a particular program, such as career speakers, which require on-site coordination. Sometimes two administrators or two counselors or an administrator and a counselor share a TA group, so one professional is always present and the other free for other responsibilities. In one school, a counselor has a "remedial group" of students who do not respond well to their initial advisor and through which recalcitrant students cycle for short periods of time.

Occasionally volunteers or non-professional staff are assigned TA groups. Each administrator will have to decide if this is feasible in a particular school. Sometimes instructional aides are certified teachers who can be as effective as TA leaders. Occasionally a school secretary or other non-professional staff member is particularly able to form relationships and carry out responsibilities such as those expected of an advisor. Volunteers from the community usually cannot serve as advisors for a TA program, simply because of time commitments required and legal considerations. They can, however, serve as co-advisors or special resource persons.

3. Where will TA groups meet? If all or most staff become advisors, the number of groups will likely exceed the number of teaching stations within the school. What other spaces can be found — the library, the stage, a spacious foyer of the school? If, for example, the assistant principal has a TA group, sufficient space must be located where the group can meet. A degree of privacy is important. More than one group meeting in the same space, even a large one such as the auditorium or cafeteria, is far from ideal, since privacy is necessary for group identity to develop.

4. When and how often will TA groups be scheduled? The frequency and length of TA meetings vary considerably from school to school. There is no standard "best" time during the school day for TA. In some schools, the entry level grade meets with advisors more often than do older students; the sixth grade may "tag in" with the advisor several times during the day — first thing in the morning, at lunchtime, and just before going home in the afternoon. Eighth graders may meet only weekly. A middle level school with a flexible time schedule can accommodate this degree of variance.

Most schools have personal development, relationship-building activities no more than once or twice a week, for about twenty-five to thirty-five minutes. Some schools schedule a short meeting with the advisor daily for official roll call, announcements, and other administrative matters, with an extended period once or twice a week for a TA activity. Other schools have a fixed time schedule daily with different kinds of activities each day and only one or two days a week devoted to a TA activity, with other days used for assemblies, intramurals, silent reading, or clubs.

If mini-courses are a part of the TA time structure, a longer time period may be required so that special interest groups such as bread-making, photography, or craft-type programs can have enough time to accomplish tasks. If TA time is first period or in the middle of the day, it may occasionally be useful to shift the schedule so that mini-courses occur last in order to continue for some groups after school. It is not always easy to call back to academics a group of young adolescents returning from a karate or cheerleading experience.

5. What budget will be required for TA activities? Some TA activities require funds. If a career day is a part of TA, will refreshments be served to guests? A school or community service project may require supplies; who buys the paint to refurbish trash cans or paint a cafeteria mural? The administrator must anticipate funds necessary for various projects and make decisions accordingly about what will be in the program .

Personnel costs may be associated with TA programs. A consultant contracted to furnish active listening skills training for advisors becomes a budget item. One or more teachers coordinating the TA program in lieu of teaching one period costs teacher time. Likewise, assigning a counselor to coordinate a TA program necessitates providing additional counseling or clerical time to offset that responsibility.

If a notebook of activities is developed, how much will it cost to put a copy in the hands of every advisor? What are the duplication costs for paper-and-pencil pieces of the program? If a "canned" program is chosen, will there be considerable costs for purchase of materials and training of teachers?

6. How will the program be presented to the school publics: parents, school board, entering students, feeder and receiving schools? Orienting everyone to the TA program, especially at its inception, is necessary. Would a newspaper article, a parent newsletter item, a presentation to the school board, a simple brochure, an explanation in the student or parent handbook, a videotape of successful TA programs, or other method be the best way to inform people about TA goals and activities? Several avenues will usually be used when launching a program. What do entering students want to know about TA programs, and how can the existence of the program reduce anxiety of a sixth grader's parent? Can high schools be encouraged to plan some sort of continuation of a TA program, at least for the first year of high school or for those at risk of not succeeding in high school? How will teachers be persuaded to participate willingly in this program, given their already over-filled day?

One principal found acceptance by offering every teacher a choice of doing lunch duty or having a TA group. Predictably, almost all teachers in the building chose a TA group, adding greatly to the success of the program, leaving lunch duty for a few teachers and the administrators. Answers to these and other questions will be required of the administrator working with the program coordinator, coordinating committee, and total staff.

9

How are parents and other community members involved?

Parents find an ongoing TA program a real boon when they seek information about their middle level students. Interested parents probably kept close contact with their child's elementary teacher, usually just one individual. Upon entering middle school, the student has several teachers and a parent wonders who to call to gain information about the school or their child's progress. The school counselor is a proper source of information, but typically the counselor has so many students assigned that this one professional cannot keep track of the progress of each student. For the counselor to report to the parent, teachers must first provide information to the counselor. Likewise, while the administrator may have much information about a few children — those who perform exceptionally well and those who require frequent disciplinary attention — to answer a parent's queries about most middle level youngsters, the administrator must first seek assistance from teachers.

The advisor who has fifteen or so young people in an advisory which meets regularly has a pretty accurate picture of how each individual is faring in school. The advisor can be the prime point of contact for a parent seeking information about a student or a school program. While the advisor will not have all the answers, he or she will be well-acquainted with the student. The advisor may not be able to give a parent an up-to-date progress report on the spot, but may request that the entire teaching team, perhaps including the counselor or the administrator, meet with the parent to adequately respond to the request. Or the advisor may direct the parent to a more appropriate source to answer the question, such as one particular teacher or a counselor with specialized knowledge. However, the advisor remains the most logical point of first contact for the parent.

Parents can provide the advisor with very valuable information about their children. Frequent home-school contacts about routine matters will be invaluable if problems arise later. If an advisor has already listened to a parent describe her daughter, a sudden change in the student's behavior will be more obvious to the advisor, and channels of communication between parent and school will already exist. Suppose, for example, a student does not understand her algebra instruction but feels great peer pressure — and perhaps parental pressure as well — to remain in the class. The fear of poor achievement and perhaps more important, losing face with her friends, may cause a noticeable behavior change in a young adolescent. The advisor can track down the cause and work with other school personnel, parents, and the student to find solutions to the problem. Especially if students stay with the same advisor all their years in the middle school, parent, advisor, and student can all come to know each other well enough for comfortable and full communication. The advisor can be a real source of security not only for the new middle level student, but also for the parent.

Parents and other members of the community can contribute to the advisory program in many specific ways.

Parents and other adults can:

— speak about their careers, hobbies, or special interests.

— volunteer to help with special events, such as field trips or weekend campouts.

— teach mini-courses, using their special talents.

— provide materials for such TA projects as public service efforts.

— mentor young people who are learning about their special interests.

— read to, listen to, talk with, or generally be a friend to a young person in a TA group who needs more attention than even the advisor can provide.

— encourage the advisor by applauding school efforts to know and value young people as individuals.

— advocate with political forces so that sufficient teacher time and resources will be made available for a successful TA program.

10

WHAT PITFALLS SHOULD YOU AVOID WHEN SETTING UP A PROGRAM?

Those experienced with TA programs caution that careful planning and preparation of advisors are keys to the success of a program. Failing to explain clearly the goals of TA and to gain full teacher acceptance of the program are probably the biggest causes of failure. Some schools have found to their sorrow that administrative fiat does not make a very successful TA program. Change is frightening to most people. Teachers, lacking earlier preparation, quite reasonably ask questions such as, "What is it I'm supposed to do? Why? Is it worth the loss of instructional time from other classes?"

Van Hoose (1991, pp. 2-3) lists seven reasons why teachers resist TA programs:

— Parents do not understand the concept and many may oppose it.

— Many administrators are not really concerned about it.

— Most teachers have had little formal preparation for ser vice as an advisor.

— Teachers do not understand the goal(s) of the endeavor.

— Advisory takes time — time that many teachers believe could be invested more effectively in preparing to teach their subject(s).

— Some teachers do not want to engage in a program that requires personal sharing.

— When it is implemented incorrectly and with little staff development and leadership, students do not provide positive feedback.

Each of those potential causes of teacher resistance needs to be considered and countered. Five of the most common reasons TA programs fail to thrive are discussed in the following paragraphs.

1. Insufficient planning time before beginning the program.

Because the concept of relationship-building as a prime advisor responsibility is new for many teachers, much planning and "selling" of the program must occur beforehand. For success, teachers, administrators, counselors, and others should feel ownership and partnership in the program. The program's contributions to the academic life of the school need to be understood. Since TA is frightening to many teachers, it should be one of the last components a middle school attempts to implement. Only after interdisciplinary teaming is in place should an advisory program be initiated.

2. Inadequate preparation of advisors.

Most teachers know how to listen and respond to students, but many lack confidence in these skills. Often advisors worry about whether they will know the right thing to say to students who bring them a concern, or whether they will recognize signs of significant student distress. Most teachers need only reinforcement of skills they already bring to the program, although some may need considerably more training. Regardless, it is foolhardy to begin a TA program without making a clear commitment in both dollars and time to providing considerable staff development.

3. Incomplete development of topics and activities for the TA program.

Teachers have so many responsibilities to fulfill during a school day that they do not need an additional preparation added to their workload. Advisors will be more eager to embrace the TA program if they understand that lesson plans are, for the most part, prepared by someone else. Often advisors go far beyond or apart from the plans provided, particularly after they gain experience, but, at least initially, provision of fairly explicit plans will relieve teacher anxiety about what actually happens during TA time.

4. Too frequent or too infrequent meetings of TA groups.

Sometimes schools become overly ambitious with their TA plans and try to have a personal development activity every day. Desirable as such activities may be, engaging students in them daily or more often than twice a week is probably inadvisable. On the other hand, meeting too infrequently does not give advisors the opportunity to know their students, nor does the group have enough time to develop cohesion. Meeting only once or twice a marking period, for example, simply does not enable students and advisors to get to know each other as individuals and participate in the kinds of activities which pay off in improved self-esteem.

5. Lack of administrative and/or counselor support for the program.

Occasionally administrators fail to see the value of a TA program, and lacking commitment, do not support it with resources and encouragement. Administrators who support TA programs realize that breaking the school down into smaller units where adults get to know students well makes other aspects of the school, such as attendance and discipline, improve. Occasionally, counselors may believe that a TA program is an encroachment on their turf. Actually, a TA program enables counselors to partner with advisors to work toward the shared goals of student growth and enhances counselor effectiveness within a school.

11

How do you keep an advisory program viable?

Just as with any other program in a school, a TA program takes care and feeding. Beginning a program is only the first step in what will be an ongoing developmental process. Teachers turn over from year to year, so periodic updating of skills of those serving as advisors is necessary. Even veteran teachers need recharging. The school administrator, the TA coordinator, and the coordinating committee should monitor the program continuously. Questions such as the following should be raised at least annually and answered by the faculty.

- Is the time of day for TA satisfactory?

- Does the program meet often enough or too often?

- How is the current method of assigning advisors and students working? Which activities work well and which don't; why?

- Are the appropriate topics being covered?

- Do teachers understand and perform their roles well as advisors? If not, what additional training or orientation is needed?

- What evidence exists to attest to the program's effectiveness?

- Do students think they are learning anything from their TA time? Is behavior improved? Are attitudes more positive?

- Have referrals to other helpers, such as counselors, increased since TA programs began? Do teachers know and use referral resources?

- Do teachers feel more a part of the school? Is everyone involved in this program in some way?

- Is the TA program worth the time and resources invested in it?

These and other such questions must be answered frequently, with changes made as necessary to insure the program's vitality. Ideally, a committee responsible for coordinating or advising about the TA program monitors constantly, recommending changes as necessary.

A TA program does not stay healthy without attention and commitment of those involved.

Formal, periodic evaluation of the program is useful. Questionnaires to elicit information from students, teachers, parents, and others can indicate the effectiveness of the program. Such questionnaires should be based on goals and objectives of the TA program and worded in terms of student behavior outcomes. Other meas-ures of school climate, such as incidents of vandalism, student and teacher attendance, rate of student and teacher transfer, numbers and severity of discipline problems, truancy, evidence of learning, attendance at school-sponsored activities, and student, parent, and community perception of the school can indicate whether or not students feel a valued part of the school.

Data collected preceding a TA program and after its beginning can be compared to see changes which may have occurred in school climate. Do students name their advisor when asked if there is someone at school they can trust and would talk to, or do they say no one there knows them or cares enough to talk to them? Do parents feel comfortable calling an advisor? How many advisors have had parent-initiated contacts, and how many advisor-initiated contacts occurred with parents? Do parents know who their child's advisor is? Have more students become involved in school activities since the program began? Has attendance improved, vandalism decreased, achievement changed, dropout rate decreased? Are more services such as free lunch and visits to clothing banks made available to students because someone cares? The TA program is by no means the sole determinant of school climate, but an effective program should produce measurable results.

There should also be evidence of the long-range effects of TA programs. Do former students make contact with their advisors? How do they fare in high school, especially the first year? Does the advisor ever follow-up with former students? Do students from one or two particular advisory groups seem to do better when they get to high school, or college?

Flexibility and teacher involvement remain the keys to a successful TA program. Teachers who remain committed to the philosophy of the program reap the best personal rewards from their efforts. As in other areas, success engenders success. Teachers who get positive feedback from their advisees are encouraged to continue their good work. The coordinating committee must listen to advisors and to students and parents to learn what is working and what needs correcting. A committee which believes the TA curriculum is sacrosanct and unyielding will greatly limit the effectiveness of the program, which must be flexible and responsive to the changing needs of young adolescents.

12

Where can you get additional help?

The resources identified below will give you more help in seeing how others view TA programs and what has been done in various schools.

The National Middle School Association has published three previous monographs which deal with advisory programs.

1. *Adviser-Advisee Programs: Why, What and How* (James, 1986) details six successful TA programs, provides a sound rationale, and offers recommendations for implementation.

2. *Guidance in Middle Level Schools: Everyone's Responsibility* (Cole, 1988) discusses the special importance of guidance services and describes the roles of various persons in the school.

3. *Treasure Chest: A Teacher Advisory Source Book* (Hoversten, Doda and Lounsbury, 1991) is an excellent resource for those planning or continuing TA programs. The three-ring binder includes general information about TA programs, with advice for advisors from teachers who have experience, as well as 120 activities organized by categories and levels. The authors urge schools to adapt and select activities. They state: "This is a source book, not a curriculum. An exemplary teacher advisory program grows more out of the student-teacher relationship than out of the materials used. The activities and content are means to ends and not ends themselves" (p. 1).

Another excellent source of information is The Center for the Education of the Young Adolescent (CEYA) at the University of Wisconsin-Platteville. A good procedure for beginning a TA program used by many middle schools in Wisconsin has been to send a planning team to the Summer Transescent Seminar, now in its eleventh year. CEYA has compiled many resources, including videotapes, on establishing TA programs and notebooks of activities developed by several schools. Included among the videotapes is one by Cole and a roomful of experienced teachers on "Teacher Advisory Programs: Beyond the First Year." Another video by Merenbloom, Cole, Jockman and Tadlock is "Features of the Middle School," which discusses the importance of a TA program.

For further information contact:

> Center for the Education of the Young Adolescent
> 128 Doudna Hall, 1 University Plaza
> Platteville, Wisconsin 53818-3099
> (608) 342-1276.

JOURNAL ARTICLES

Andes, J. (1988, May). Increased academic achievement through advisement. *NASSP Bulletin, 72* (508), 113-114.

Brough, J. (1985, August). Teacher as counselor: Some considerations. *Middle School Journal, XVI* (4), 4, 8-9.

Cole, C. (1990, November). 2001: A middle school odyssey. *Middle School Journal, 22* (2), 3-6.

Connors, N. and Irvin, J. (1989, May). Is "middle-schoolness" an indicator of excellence? *Middle School Journal, 20* (5), 12-15.

George, P. (1990, February). From junior high to middle school — principals' perspectives. *Middle School Journal, 21* (5), 31-33.

Gill, J. and Read, J. (1990, May). Experts comment on Adviser/Advisee programs. *Middle School Journal, 21* (5), 31-33.

Hash, V. and Vernon, A. (1987, August). Helping early adolescents deal with stress. *Middle School Journal, 18* (4), 22-23.

Mac Iver, D. (1990, February). Meeting the needs of young adolescents: Advisory group, interdisciplinary teaching teams, and school transition programs. *Kappan, 71* (6), 458-464.

Maeroff, G. (1990, March). Getting to know a good middle school: Shoreham-Wading River. *Kappan, 71* (7), 505-511.

Myrick, R., Highland, M., and Highland, B. (1986, May). Preparing teachers to be advisers. *Middle School Journal, XVII* (3), 15-16.

Nattermann, J. (1988, September). Teachers as advisers: Complementing school guidance program. *NASSP Bulletin, 72* (509), 121-123.

Strahan, D. (1989, November). Disconnected and disruptive students. *Middle School Journal, 21* (2), 1-6.

BOOKS

Amatea, E. (1975) *The Yellow Brick Road.* Tallahassee, FL: Career Education Center, Florida State University.

Canfield, J. and H. Wells (1976). *100 Ways to Enhance Self-Concept in the Classroom.* Englewood Cliffs, NJ: Prentice-Hall, Inc. Research Press.

Timmerman, T. (1975). *Growing Up Alive.* Amherst, MA: Mandala Press.

References Cited

Cisneros, S. (1991). *Woman Hollering Creek and Other Stories*. New York: Random House.

Cole, C. (1988). *Guidance in the Middle School: Everyone's Responsibility*. Columbus, Ohio: National Middle School Association.

Glasser, W. (1986). *Control Theory in the Classroom*. New York: Harper and Row Publishers.

Glasser, W. (1990). *The Quality School*. New York: Harper and Row Publishers.

Hoversten, C., Doda, N., and Lounsbury, J. (1991). *Treasure Chest: A Teacher Advisory Source Book*. Columbus, Ohio: National Middle School Association.

Hutchins, D. and Cole, C (1991). *Helping Relationships and Strategies* (2nd edition). Monterey, CA: Brooks/Cole.

James, M. (1986). *Adviser-Advisee Programs: Why, What and How*. Columbus, Ohio: National Middle School Association.

Kozol, J. (1991). *Savage Inequalities*. New York: Crown Publishers.

Van Hoose, J. (1991). The ultimate goal: AA across the day. *Midpoints, 2* (1). Columbus, Ohio: National Middle School Association.

To be successful advisors, teachers must be able to jettison an authoritarian attitude toward their students. A discussion of thoughts and feelings does not require the teacher to know the "right" answer in the same way as does a discussion of a mathematics procedure, where presumably there is a correct answer. While the teacher never abdicates the classroom management of the TA group, the direction of the discussion and the leadership of the group may not always rest with the advisor. This does not mean that inappropriate topics may be introduced by students at will, nor does it presuppose that the advisor ignores inappropriate behavior. But the traditional role of the teacher always in charge changes, partly because of the small numbers involved and partly because of the task to be accomplished, relationship-building.

Treasure Chest: A Teacher Advisory Source Book, explains, "The more the advisor can become a regular member of the group sharing in appropriate activities, the better. The advisor must not, of course, overdo involvement and dominate, but establishing an atmosphere of relative intimacy is essential" (Hoversten, Doda, and Lounsbury, 1991, p.7). The advisor/advisee relationship may be analogous to that which develops between a coach and a team, a sponsor and a club, a youth minister and a youth group, a band director and band members. For many TA activities, the teacher becomes involved more as a participant than as the person in charge. In some ways it is inappropriate to refer to the advisor as a *teacher* since the label implies a role different from that of an *advisor*.

Sample Activity

Every student and the advisor get a grid similar to a Bingo sheet with phrases descriptive of summer activities such as "went to the beach" or "played on a team." Each person in the TA group, including the advisor, moves around the room collecting signatures in appropriate blocks, presumably learning names and finding interests in common. To conclude the activity, the advisor can draw the group together to recount good books read, or tourist attractions visited, or new family members acquired, thus providing closure and a sense of group identity.   — continued

---